SLP

TIMBERLAND REGIONAL LIBRARY

‖‖‖‖‖‖‖‖‖‖‖‖‖‖‖

A20015 909110

DEC 1 1 '96   OLYMPIA

‖‖‖‖‖‖‖‖‖‖‖‖

P9-DUC-269

Timberland Regional Library
Service Center
415 Airdustrial Way S.W.
Olympia, WA 98501

Gardens
OF
ALCATRAZ

OFFICALLY WITHDRAWN FROM
TIMBERLAND REGIONAL LIBRARY

NOV 2 6 1996

Gardens of ALCATRAZ

ESSAYS BY

JOHN HART, RUSSELL A. BEATTY
& MICHAEL BOLAND

PHOTOGRAPHS BY

ROY EISENHARDT

GOLDEN GATE NATIONAL PARKS ASSOCIATION
SAN FRANCISCO, CALIFORNIA

COPYRIGHT ©1996 BY GOLDEN GATE NATIONAL PARKS ASSOCIATION
All rights reserved. No part of this book may be reproduced in any form without written permisssion from the publisher. For information, contact Golden Gate National Parks Association, Building 201, Fort Mason, San Francisco, CA 94123.

"THE ROCK: THE CURIOUS GREENING OF ALCATRAZ" ©1996 BY JOHN HART
UNLESS OTHERWISE NOTED, ALL PHOTOGRAPHS ©1996 BY ROY EISENHARDT

Historical photographs on pp. 4, 6, 7, 8, 10, 12, 18, 31, 35, and 74 are from the National Park Service archives, Golden Gate National Recreation Area; p. 22, from the *San Francisco Chronicle*. Contemporary photographs are courtesy Brenda Tharp (p. 5), Kathy O'Hara (p. 11), and Mindy Manville (p. 37).

LIBRARY OF CONGRESS CATALOG CARD NUMBER 95-80208
ISBN 1-883869-17-X (PAPER), ISBN 1-883869-19-6 (CLOTH)

Special thanks to Michael Boland for his assistance with photo selection, plant identification, and project facilitation; to all three essay authors for their generosity of spirit and help throughout the project; to photographer Roy Eisenhardt for his many trips to the island in search of exactly the right flowering plant; to Ron Lutsko and Robin Menigoz for their 1992 study of the plants of Alcatraz; and to the National Park Service interpretive staff for their time, information, and concern for the island of Alcatraz itself.

Golden Gate National Parks Association is a non-profit membership organization established to support the education, conservation, interpretation, and research programs of Golden Gate National Recreation Area. To learn more about our activities, contact us at the address above or telephone (415) 776-0693.

Editor, Susan Tasaki
Designer, Jami Spittler
Production assistant, Sterling Larrimore
Map, Jami Spittler, based on 1993 GGNPA Alcatraz site survey diagram.

Printed on recycled paper in Hong Kong through Global Interprint, Inc.

LEFT: ICE PLANT

COVER: FUCHSIA; INSET: DETAIL, EADWEARD MUYBRIDGE PHOTOGRAPH, CA. 1870, COURTESY NPS ARCHIVES, GGNRA

FRONTIS: BERMUDA BUTTERCUP (*Oxalis pes-caprae*)
PAGE 87: ALCATRAZ ISLAND, EVENING
PAGE 96: DETAIL, *Agave americana*

THE GOLDEN GATE PROVIDES A DISTANT BACKDROP FOR ARTICHOKE PLANTS.

The Gardens of Alcatraz

DELPHINE HIRASUNA

The hundreds of thousands of people who ride the ferry across San Francisco Bay to Alcatraz each year rarely notice or remember the island's flowers and shrubs. It is the federal penitentiary, bleak and imposing, that draws their attention and haunts their memories. The cold walls of the isolation cells. The ruins of the warden's house. The stories of the gangsters. Little wonder that the gardens of Alcatraz are barely noticed.

But the island's curious mix of plants—stately iris and diminutive grape hyacinths, spiky agaves and artichokes, scattered fruit trees, bursts of California poppies—have their own intriguing stories to tell. Planted by successive generations of inhabitants, from Civil War soldiers and civilian criminals to the families of officers and guards, they provide clues to the aspirations and yearnings of those who once lived here. In the straggly remains of a rose garden, you can almost picture the Victorian wives of army officers taking afternoon tea in the shade of the citadel. Elsewhere on the island, gladiolus and narcissus bloom in lasting tribute to the prisoners who tenderly cared for them more than a half-century ago.

On "the Rock," little grew uninvited or untended. Only human tenacity enabled plants to flourish. In this sense, the gardens of Alcatraz are testaments to the human spirit, to the desire to create life and beauty even in a forbidding environment. Perhaps this above all is what makes these gardens so inspiring—and so touching.

Although largely neglected since the prison was shut down in 1963, these plants have shown remarkable adaptability and endurance. Nature has exerted its own direction and has been startlingly successful. Many trees, plants, and shrubs have continued to thrive, outgrowing their original boundaries and wildly intermingling with one another.

Perspectives on specific aspects of the gardens of Alcatraz are presented in the three essays that follow. John Hart considers the island's human history. Russell A. Beatty focuses on the plants and those who tended them. Finally, Michael Boland leads us on a tour of the various gardens and offers an informed opinion on what they could symbolize in the larger realm of environmental concerns. Our appreciation and respect for this uniquely American treasure are enhanced by their views.

You will likely take comfort in the power and perseverance of the natural order, and look fondly on the old rose bushes, gnarled trees, and other green, living things that now cover and soften the face of the island. After touring the prison cellhouse, it is reassuring to stroll around the island's gardens as a reminder of all that is hopeful about humanity.

The Rock Garden

THE CURIOUS GREENING
OF ALCATRAZ

ABOVE: NASTURTIUMS *(Tropaeolum majus)* AND IVY OVERGROWING DRAIN
PREVIOUS: CHASMANTHE *(Chasmanthe floribunda)*

The Rock Garden

THE CURIOUS GREENING OF ALCATRAZ

—

JOHN HART

They call it "the Rock" for good reason. From a distance, and in the distance of our minds, Alcatraz Island is an archetype of hardness, coldness, grayness, sterility. It is an island of shipwrecks and navigational warnings, of soldiers and ponderous iron cannon, of desperate prisoners and anonymous guards. All business. Hardly anyone lived on this twenty-two-acre spot of land by choice. But many people lived here by necessity, and they did what people so often do to enliven bleak surroundings: in this place of defense and punishment, they planted gardens.

In 1963, about one hundred years after the first of these gardeners came, the last of them left; but their plantings remained, and thrived. Today, three decades after maintenance ended, the plants that once grew in narrow beds and hedges have covered much of the island in a thicket of green and blossom. Alcatraz is still gray, still cold, still battered by the wind, but today it is very far from barren. A whole assembly of plants from around the world—with just a few of local origin—has formed a novel and evolving community, an ecosystem-in-training.

ALCATRAZ ALONE

This modern blooming is not in any sense a restoration. In a state of nature, the island was a bare little camel's back of land, about a quarter of a mile long and five hundred feet across, rising in a double summit some 140 feet above the tide. One long side, facing the Golden Gate, was plucked at by currents and pummeled by the wind; the opposite, inland-

facing shore was only comparatively sheltered. Even on the leeward side, apparently, nothing grew taller than a bush. The Miwok Indians of Marin County to the north and the Ohlone of San Francisco to the south may have visited the island for seabird eggs, but there is no evidence that any band lived there. When the Spanish arrived in the 1770s, they were equally disinclined to occupy the island. For people, there were obviously better places to live: in fact, almost any place was better.

Alcatraz suited wildlife, however, just fine. Seals and sea lions hauled out on its shores, and birds gathered on its heights. Western gulls and other seabirds nested. Brown pelicans probably roosted in large numbers. Three species of cormorants, sleek, dark-feathered diving birds, used the island for a specific purpose: after their underwater hunts, they spread their wings to dry in its all-but-constant wind. So numerous were the birds that the rock was white with their guano.

In 1775, Lieutenant Juan Manuel de Ayala sailed into San Francisco Bay and visited a rugged barren island. "It proved so arid and steep that there was not even a boat-harbor there; I named the island *de los Alcatraces* because of their [birds] being so plentiful there." *Alcatraces* is traditionally translated "pelicans"; a newer interpretation renders the key word as "cormorants."[1]

Ayala's description fit Alcatraz well, but it would also have suited Yerba Buena Island, the larger and more prominent landmass to the east, and Yerba Buena was almost certainly the original *Isla de los Alcatraces*.

BRENDA THARP

ABOVE: GULL EGGS

OPPOSITE: ALCATRAZ, CIRCA 1850

It was in 1827 that a British navy surveyor moved the name to today's site. Perhaps the Britisher, Captain Frederick Beechey, wanted to highlight a feature that quite overshadowed Yerba Buena from a naval point of view.

For Alcatraz had one undeniable value: strategic location. If some omnipotent military board had been assigned to place an island exactly where it would best command San Francisco and its harbor, this island would have been the result. You can almost imagine it being towed this way, nudged that way, like the great ship it resembles, and finally anchored

exactly where it would do the most good: where guns placed on it could sweep the inner portal of the Golden Gate, the door into one of the great natural harbors of the world.

THE FORTRESS

Shortly after the American takeover in 1846, surveys and studies for fortification began; in 1853, an officer with the wonderful name of Zealous Bates Tower arrived on the island to carry them out. To Tower and his superiors, the island as found was only raw material. In the first of many modifications, engineers scraped and blasted at the shores to produce daunting cliffs at those points where nature had not already provided them. On the flattened south summit of the island rose a fortified barracks, or citadel. In between, on terraces excavated about sixty feet above the water, were the gun emplacements themselves. One fortified road, climbing from a dock on the inland side, connected the levels.

Alcatraz at this stage belonged to the generation of forts known as the "Third System." The typical Third System structure was a single building with cannon mounted on the roof and projecting from slits in the walls; Fort Point on the San Francisco side of the Golden Gate, completed in 1861, is an example. But on Alcatraz the components were scattered; the island itself served as the "building," and, indeed, soon began to resemble one. Walls, revetments, parapets of brick and sandstone were everywhere, protecting not only particular structures, roads, and gun emplacements but also the very substance of the land. This Rock, built of a blue-tinged, seamy sandstone so soft that iron spikes could be driven into it, is anything but a Gibraltar; it is quite unsuitable for construction, and, once disturbed, prone to sliding. It had to be armored against gravity as well as against incoming fire.

Alcatraz got its first temporary guns in 1854 and was fully garrisoned in 1859. Even that late, it was the only permanent fortification west of the Mississippi River. With the coming of the Civil War, its armaments multiplied. By the end of that struggle, batteries bristled all along the southwest shore of the island, and gunnery terraces curled partway around its northeastern end. The commanding officer of the day estimated that these pieces, if discharged at once, would send almost 7,000 pounds of shot across the water.

Location made the isle of guard ideal also for a navigation light. The lighthouse that opened here in 1854 was, like the fort, the first of its kind on the Pacific Coast. A cunningly constructed "third-order" Fresnel lens of crystal prisms concentrated the light of an oil flame and sent it beaming nineteen miles out to sea, drawing ships inward through the proper channel and warning them off the island itself. For foggy nights, the island carried a thousand-pound fog bell, struck by an automated thirty-pound hammer.

RIGHT: ORIGINAL LIGHTHOUSE, CIRCA 1900
OPPOSITE: ORDNANCE YARD, CIRCA 1868

AN ALCATRAZ GARDEN PARTY, CIRCA 1870

EADWEARD MUYBRIDGE

Alcatraz at this stage was a stony place indeed, almost devoid of soil. But non-utilitarian gardening had already begun. By the end of the Civil War, people were excavating sockets in the rock of Alcatraz, filling them with imported earth, and planting ornamental gardens. In front of the brick citadel a formal garden was laid out, with picket fences, masonry paths, and ornamental stacks of cannonballs. Early photographer Eadweard Muybridge photographed the officers' families there. Another garden, smaller and more sheltered, appeared along the main access road just below the island crown.

THE AGE OF SOIL

The sculpting of Alcatraz resumed after the Civil War. One of the engagements of that war— the successful Union attack on Fort Pulaski, Georgia—had shown that the Third System guns and defenses were out of date. Protective walls of brick and masonry could not hold up against increasingly powerful guns. The emplacements on Alcatraz, hemmed in between cliffs below and cliffs above, were particularly vulnerable: incoming fire striking the slopes behind them would rake the emplacements with rock fragments and ricochets. The new thinking required that guns be set in wide spaces and protected not by rigid walls but by mounds of soft, absorbent earth.

Accordingly, beginning in 1869, the narrow gun terraces were widened backwards into the hill. The material scraped and blasted from the slopes behind was simply spilled over the cliffs in front, burying the older defensive works and at some points sliding on down to tidewater. Several original coves were thus filled in, and the coast began to assume the regular shiplike contour of today. At the southeast end of Alcatraz, the leveling process went even farther: the whole southern third of the island was beveled away for a parade ground. By 1890, nearly every square yard of the ancient island surface had either been cut away or buried in fill.

The new defense plan required vast imports of soil. It came by the bargeload, mostly from Angel Island. With it came seeds of plants now common on the smaller island, including coyote brush, blue elderberry, wild blackberry, and perhaps California poppies (though a strain of poppy would have been native here). Insects and rodents not formerly found on the island came along for the ride. Still other plants were introduced to control erosion on the vulnerable new slopes. The army tried alfalfa, barley, clover, and actual blocks of sod brought over from mainland meadows. Later on, ivy, honeysuckle, and ice plant would be used.

In the early 1880s, the smaller formal garden in the lee of the citadel gave way to a row of three

OPPOSITE: FUCHSIA

BELOW: OFFICERS' COTTAGES, CIRCA 1893

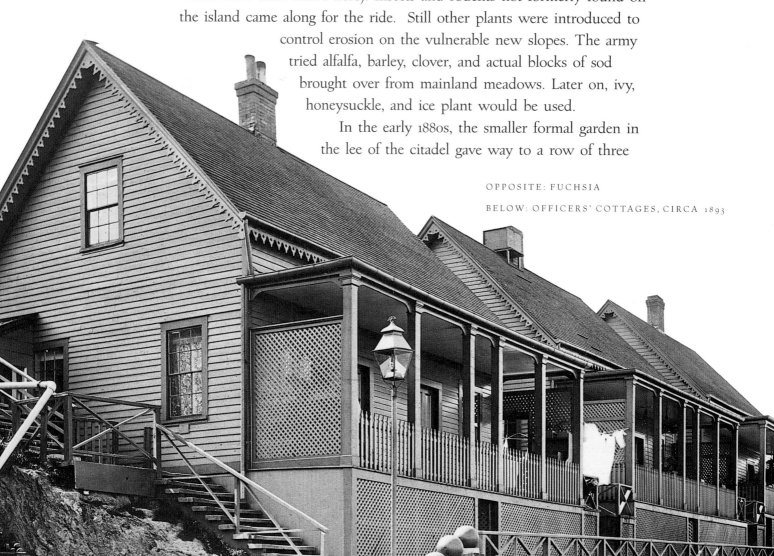

officers' cottages in Gothic style; each of these had its own garden plot, as well as windowboxes and planters. The lighthouse-keeper of the day, whose home formed an offset fourth at the end of this officers' row, was an avid gardener as well. Through all the changes to come, plants in this part of the island were lovingly tended.

The species planted, or at least the ones that thrived, displayed a certain kind of toughness. In this foggy and maritime climate, neither heat-tolerance nor frost-tolerance mattered, but plants had to endure all-but-continuous wind. Water being at a premium, they also had to tolerate summer drought, though ameliorated by the moisture of fog. In this regime, lawns were a luxury paid for with endless care. The plants that flourished came from the Mediterranean, Mexico, and—a remarkable number of species—from the southern hemisphere: South Africa, Australia, and the southern parts of South America. Valerian or heliotrope, a tall herb

with showy pink flowers, grew originally on rocky sites around the Mediterranean; the shiny-leafed mirror plant, a hedge species, on sea-cliffs in New Zealand; the adaptable agave or century plant, a desert plant that thrives in moderate climates, in western Mexico (it appears first in 1890s pictures of officers' row). Fuchsia, a plant of the New World tropics, did equally well on Alcatraz.

FROM POST TO PRISON

Alcatraz was a prison from the moment it was a fort: among the first regular occupants in 1859 were men confined for various military infractions. From then on, the island's role as a place of confinement tended always to grow. In 1861, it was designated the official military prison for the Department of the Pacific. During the Civil War, it was a convenient place to house active rebels; army men who would not confirm their allegiance to the national government; and Southern sympathizers whom we would now call political prisoners. (Some were locked up for celebrating the assassination of President Abraham Lincoln—and indeed were probably safer inside than out.) At first the men were confined in the

basement of the small guardhouse near the dock; but very soon improvised housing spread over the island, and would eventually occupy fully a third of it. Among the inmates were bewildered captives from the western Indian Wars, including Hopis, Apaches, and Modocs. For these high desert natives to be thrust onto this damp, gray, coastal island must have been a potent punishment in itself.

For one hundred years, prisoners were the main labor force on the island. They built things and tore them down. Over the decades, stone by stone and wheelbarrow by wheelbarrow, they moved thousands of tons of the substance of Alcatraz. As prison uses spread, ever more of the old gun-related works—revetments, parapets, caponiers, barbettes—disappeared under masses of shattered rock or imported soil. And on those new surfaces, the gardens—often planted by prisoners, largely tended by prisoners—spread.

As late as the turn of the century, the fiction was maintained that Alcatraz the prison was an adjunct to Alcatraz the fort. But with guns growing ever-more powerful, their ranges ever longer, the defense of the Golden Gate now depended on batteries at its outer entrance, facing the ocean; a gun platform within the strait no longer had much value. By 1901, the island had not a single piece of artillery in service.

In 1907, the army made it official. The "Post on Alcatraz Island" was no more; instead, the whole property became the "United States Military Prison,

ABOVE: GULLS ON THE SHORELINE
OPPOSITE: VIEW ALONG MAIN ROAD ASCENDING THE ISLAND, CIRCA 1900

Pacific Branch." In 1909, the handsome old brick citadel was torn down to make way for the great cellhouse that is still the culmination and the symbol of Alcatraz. Parts of the older building were salvaged. One granite portal marked the doorway of the new commandant's office, and the whole first floor of the citadel—sunk below ground level but formerly surrounded by an open moat—was retained as a true basement and foundation floor. These now-lightless spaces would briefly serve for solitary confinement. When new, the cellhouse was the largest reinforced-concrete structure in the world. A new lighthouse had to be built, too, so that its beams could clear its looming neighbor.

A KINDER, GENTLER ALCATRAZ?

From the beginning, the army seems to have been a little bashful about its prominent prison, "Uncle Sam's Devil's Island." People wondered whether this necessary function should be carried out on such a central, spectacular site. In 1915, when the great Panama-Pacific International Exposition was held on the facing shore of San Francisco, Alcatraz was a grim but unacknowledged presence. In the five-volume official history of the fair and its site, the island is mentioned not once.[2]

In that same year, in an effort to lighten the tone, the military prison was renamed the "Disciplinary Barracks," with a new emphasis on rehabilitation. ("The object is to achieve a perfect character," read a slogan stenciled on the walls.)[3] The army invited reporters onto the island and welcomed publicity about gentler aspects of the scene—including, of course, the gardens, blooming again after the disruptive construction period.

In 1918, a letter in the Alcatraz newsletter "The Rock" praised the army's landscaping: "The visitor who comes here expects to find a barren rock, but as he strolls over it he is sur-

ABOVE: DWARF GLADIOLUS
OPPOSITE: NARCISSUS HYBRID

ABOVE: NATIVE RYE *(Elymus triticoides)* GRASSLAND
OPPOSITE: EUCALYPTUS LEAVES

prised to find roses in bloom, sweet peas, lilies, and a large variety of other flowers in all their beauty and fragrance. . . . In this way barren wastes are converted into garden spots, and ugliness is transformed into beauty."[4]

In the 1920s, the beautification campaign grew more strenuous. The relatively modest commandant's house on officers' row was replaced with a massive Mission Revival structure; several other buildings were added in the same curvilinear style. In 1924, the California Spring Blossom and Wild Flower Association took on the island as a project, planting not only flowers and bushes but also the first considerable number of trees: eucalyptus, cypress, pine, and even some giant sequoia (none of the latter survived).

This was perhaps the heyday of Alcatraz the managed garden. The island was full of prisoners, but most of them, in for fairly minor offenses, were given the run of the island. Preferred prisoners, called "Disciples," and lower-class ones, called "Numbers," were everywhere, writes historian John A. Martini: "working on the dock, gardening, pruning trees, painting buildings, constructing new seawalls, or simply walking."[5]

But the army was still less than proud of its notorious prison, and the cost of maintaining the outpost was starting to hurt. Every few years, there was talk of closure. Meanwhile, Prohibition and then the Depression arrived, and with them an era of infamous criminals. The authorities wanted a "super-maximum security" lockup for these "public enemies." In 1933, the island passed to an agency that regarded a grim image and a prominent location as deterrent assets, not liabilities: the federal Bureau of Prisons.

WESTSIDE GARDENS BELOW THE CELLHOUSE, CIRCA 1946

THE UNITED STATES PENITENTIARY, ALCATRAZ ISLAND

As it entered the most notorious period of its history, the island was once again updated. Though the alterations this time around were more subtle, they completely altered the mood of the place. The flat iron bars in the cellhouse were replaced with cylindrical ones of case-hardened steel. Dozens of odd gaps, tunnels, and hiding places, left over from the varied structures on the island, were plugged with concrete and metal. Gun towers rose and barbed wire fences stretched from salt water to salt water. On the shores, ominous signs warned boats to keep their distance. One of the first prisoners in the new Alcatraz, a man named Robert Moxon who had done a separate stint in army days, exclaimed on arrival: "Christ, they've sure changed this joint."[6] The rock was now, truly, The Rock.

For all that, Alcatraz the prison was in some ways oddly luxurious. It was not, for instance, overcrowded: customers as tough as Al Capone and "Doc" Barker were kept strictly one to a cell. The food, for institutional fare, was apparently good; Warden James A. Johnston saw decent cooking as a cheap way of keeping down discontent and trouble. Yet the psychological grimness was real. The great complaint was not the cold, not the wind that sounded at the walls all day, not even the tantalizing view of city lights, but the overpowering *grayness*.

To fight that, Warden Johnston had the larger prison spaces painted in lively colors.[7] And there was a world outside. Twice a day, the prisoners who were not specially confined for misbehavior descended the slopes on the seaward side of the island to work in two industrial buildings near the northern tip. They did laundry for military bases around the bay; they sewed uniforms; they constructed deck mats and, during World War II, submarine nets. And, even in the federal prison years, they tended gardens. In fact, they conquered new ground for horticulture: it appears to have been during the federal prison era that gardens occupied the wind-

ward side of the island, on the slopes below the cellhouse. Once established, a surprising variety of plants did well here, including even some
fruit trees.

THE LIMBO YEARS

Under the Bureau of Prisons, as before, Alcatraz was expensive to
run. In fact, it was the government's most costly lockup. As always,
everything consumed on the island, even water, had to be brought in by
boat. The buildings, many of them now a century old, needed constant
upkeep. Even the 1912 cellhouse was corroding in the moist salt air. Talk
of closure mounted. In 1963, after a couple of well-publicized and embar-
rassing escape attempts, U.S. Attorney General Robert F. Kennedy pulled
the plug. Obsolete as a fort and obsolete as a prison, what would
Alcatraz now become?

After the departure of the prisoners, the federal government offered the
island to the state and then to local governments, as specified by law.
Astonishingly, there were no takers. The next step: auction the property
off to the highest private bidder.

That stirred a lot of belated attention. One group that was watching in
those early days of Native American activism was the Bay Area Council of
American Indians. In 1964, a delegation occupied the island, citing an 1868
treaty according to which members of the Sioux tribe not living on reser-
vations had a right to homestead surplus federal property. The surprised
but amiable caretaker told the landing party, "Well, I guess if you want it,
you can have it."[8] His superiors didn't agree, and the group allowed itself
to be chased away four hours later, having reaped for its cause the front-
page coverage it sought.

The impending disposal also caught the attention of San Francisco's
supervisors and mayor, who asked for more time to arrive at a plan.
Public hearings were held and a long list of ideas advocated. Gigantic stat-
ues were particularly popular. In the end, though, the city fell in with a

VIEW THROUGH A CORRODING WINDOW FRAME, LAUNDRY BUILDING

V. MAGGIORA, SAN FRANCISCO CHRONICLE

"INDIANS OF ALL TRIBES" IN THE OCCUPATION'S EARLY DAYS

notably undistinguished plan by Texas millionaire Lamar Hunt to build a commercial theme park in celebration of space travel.

People who originally had no idea what they wanted done with Alcatraz knew instantly that *this* was not what they wanted. A citizens' campaign roared to life and soon focused around a plan to make the island part of a Golden Gate National Recreation Area consisting of former military lands.

But the local Native American leaders were not done with Alcatraz. Ever since the action of 1964, they had been wondering whether the island might literally become a cultural center for the tribes. Coincidentally, a building they used in San Francisco had just burned down. Motives combined to produce one of the most dramatic episodes in the history of Alcatraz, the Indian occupation of 1969-1971.

After a couple of false starts, Indians landed on the island on November 20, 1969, and this time they stayed. The time was right for attention to their grievances about government policy, and attention came. Large segments of the press and public rallied around the occupiers. The Department of the Interior negotiated with them as equals. At the high point of their influence, the Indians received a verbal offer of land at Fort Mason on the mainland—the precious waterfront area now known as Fort Mason Center—and turned it down.[9] In the internal debate between those who wished to use the island as a pulpit or a bargaining chip and those who wanted to live there permanently, the literalists had won.

From there it was all downhill. The government removed the water barge that served the island, and attempted to cut off power. On June 1, 1970, fires broke out and gutted the warden's house, the lighthouse-keeper's quarters, the doctor's house (last survivor of the 1880s officers' row), and the Mission Revival officers' club. The demoralized "garrison" hung on but dwindled from month to month. Finally, a year later, federal marshals removed the few people remaining. Alcatraz had proved to be a superb place to make a point but a difficult place to make a home.

The Native American occupiers do not appear to have planted anything on the island, but their struggle left marks on it. Now, when you approach the wharf, the block-lettered "U.S. Penitentiary" sign is paired with fading, poignant scrawls: "Indians Welcome," "Indian Land." And the occupation gave the island something it had not formerly possessed: ruins. The shell of the warden's house—in truth, more interesting to look at than the house itself—is, with lighthouse and cellhouse, a symbol of Alcatraz today. After the trespassers were removed, and before the National Park Service arrived, the interim custodian, the General Services Administration, added to the archeology by knocking down the apartment buildings that stood on the parade ground.

THE PARK

The Native American seizure and occupation had the effect of raising the island's stock enormously. For the first time in history, someone had wanted to live there! In 1972, the vast Golden Gate National Recreation Area was authorized, and Alcatraz was almost its centerpiece, an ambiguous jewel.

With the arrival of the National Park Service, the island of rapid and repeated transformations entered a quiet period of its history. The new managers were in no hurry to make changes; indeed, they had no idea what changes would be appropriate. In the General Management Plan of 1980, issued after months of meetings and hearings, the service made one basic (and controversial) decision: that the great cellhouse, the grim Acropolis of the island, should remain. Elsewhere, maintenance has been limited to retaining a state of "arrested decay."

Another promise of the 1980 plan—increased public access—is slowly being fulfilled; in 1994, the new Agave Trail opened the way to the island's southeast point. But western gulls and black-crowned night herons have priority: in spring and summer, when they are nesting and raising their young, large areas of the island are closed.

While buildings deteriorate, plants grow. Perhaps the most dramatic change since 1963 is the spreading exuberance of green, especially toward

INTERIOR OF THE OFFICERS' CLUB, CARPETED IN RED VALERIAN

the southern end of the island. Fuchsia hangs down the retaining walls along the access road. Valerian runs wild in the burned-out shell of the warden's house. The rounded ruins of apartment houses on the parade ground become domes of mirror plant. The southwest slope below the cellhouse is a jungle of elderberry, coyote brush, privet escaped from hedges, and more mirror plant. Look closely, and you'll spot fig trees, apple trees, and a greenhouse disappearing in the growth. Old-fashioned geraniums and old Asian roses bloom in their old places.

THE FUTURE OF THE ROCK GARDEN

What will happen to the strange assemblage of plants that has greened and softened the hard-edged forms of Alcatraz?

If left strictly alone, ecology tells us, disturbed land tends to revert to what it was before disturbance. Today's dominant species give way to tomorrow's, drifting subtly but implacably toward a climax state dictated by climate, by soil, and by other specific characteristics of a site. An abandoned orchard becomes, perhaps, a live oak grove. But how will these processes play out on an island where even the soil is a human import? Where almost all plants are exotic? And where the most nearly native species (the ones brought over from Angel Island) are plants of the "pioneer" type, destined to succeed to—what?

What, meanwhile, will the National Park Service be doing? The plants of Alcatraz are at the same time a changing natural system and a historical collection. Should some parts of this living scene be deliberately frozen? How much of Alcatraz should be treated, still, as a garden?

"They've sure changed this joint," the returning prisoner remarked. That could be the motto of this island, shaped and reshaped, planted and replanted, built and rebuilt on the rubble of its own rapid history. Now it enters a long afternoon in which change is gentler, slower, but no less profound. What Alcatraz will be in another few generations is hard to imagine. "They" will be changing this joint for a very long time to come.

Long, Enduring Patterns

GARDENERS AND THEIR PLANTS

ABOVE: TORCH PLANT *(Aloe arborescens)*

PREVIOUS: *Rosa* 'GARDENIA'

Long, Enduring Patterns

GARDENERS AND THEIR PLANTS

———

RUSSELL A. BEATTY

Too often, plants and gardens are considered only in visual terms, as objects or places of beauty. Certainly, much of the enjoyment we receive from visiting beautiful gardens and landscapes comes from the beauty of the plants and spectacular flowers, trees with interesting sculptural forms, soothing carpets of green. But greater benefit than mere aesthetics can be realized when we learn some of the deeper meanings of a garden and the process of its creation.

The story of the gardens of Alcatraz is a compelling account of men and plants brought together on an island uninhabitable by either. Like their keepers, the plants brought to the island over the past 140 years became prisoners too, isolated from the well-tended gardens of the mainland on a wind-swept hump in one of the world's windiest gaps. As the human residents "inside" discovered, only those that could adapt, survived. Today, these plants are a living history of an island in constant change. They tell the other story of Alcatraz—the human and humane story of individual and group efforts to bring a bit of beauty to a grim place; of fashion in plant selection through the years; of survival and adaptation to an uncom-

promising environment; of rich new ecosystems created where none existed before; and of the therapeutic solace found in caring for plants in a
place where little compassion existed.

GARDENERS ON THE ROCK

Several circa-1870 photographs, taken during the height of the island's
military occupation, show an elaborate garden on the south side of the
citadel. Typically Victorian in its layout—chock full of
flowers, fences dripping with roses, and irrigated
by canvas hoses from underground cisterns—this garden clearly demonstrates
a desire to bring civility and beauty
to an otherwise-barren fortress.
Initially, soil was brought from
Angel Island to create planting beds. Such
an effort necessitated small, compact gardens located
in spots sheltered from the strong westerly winds. In addition
to gardens planted by the officers' families, the army developed a
progressive vocational program aimed at prisoner rehabilitation. In
September 1917, their newsletter, "The Rock," reported that a training program had begun in which eight men were studying to become gardeners.
Their efforts were reported in a March 1918 issue: they had cut deep holes
into the rock, filled them with soil, and planted roses, sweet peas, and
lilies.

Public and internal disapproval of the island's appearance inspired
more extensive beautification efforts. Lawns of clover and bluegrass were
planted around the officers' quarters—tiny patches but nonetheless an
improvement. In the fall of 1923 and spring of 1924, the California Spring
Blossom and Wild Flower Association mounted an aggressive campaign to
beautify Alcatraz as well as Yerba Buena and Angel islands. Many plants
did not survive due to a shortage of water and lack of adequate mainte-

EADWEARD MUYBRIDGE

ABOVE: CITADEL GARDEN, CIRCA 1870

OPPOSITE: CALLA (*Zantedeschia aethiopica*)

Aptenia cordifolia DRAPES A RETAINING WALL

nance. But with moisture from summer fog and their own adaptability, some endured. Army photographs show eucalyptus and cypress, ice plant covering the slopes, and century plants along the south side of the island, lining what was known by the curious name of "Lover's Lane." (One cannot conceive of a less romantic plant than the spiky agave, but this was Alcatraz!)

Prison Bureau employees arriving in early 1934 were greeted by an unexpected riot of color spilling down the rock slopes and terraces, blankets of pink-flowered ice plant, a beautiful rose garden and greenhouse, and smaller gardens scattered throughout the island. This "Persian carpet" must have helped ease their fears of the life they anticipated on the Rock.

One of these early arrivals was a man who would continue and expand on the army's garden legacy. Freddie Reichel, secretary to Warden Johnston from 1934 to 1941, was so impressed with the gardens left by the army that he committed his free time to their care and to expanding the plantings. In correspondence (circa 1978), Reichel detailed an account of the gardens and his efforts over seven years to improve them.

"I knew . . . that it would be impossible to maintain all that glory . . . but I resolved then and there to try to find some time in my . . . long days for the relaxation afforded by the raising of plants for others to tend and the development of areas by myself."

He took over "the rose garden, the greenhouse, the slope behind my quarters, and the small, flat garden near the Post Exchange." Though he had little horticultural experience, Reichel became an expert self-taught gardener through his love of plants and his dedication to improving Alcatraz. From his island isolation, he enlisted advice, help, and plants from a group of experts that reads like a *Who's Who* of California horticulture: Kate Sessions of San Diego, Hugh Evans of Los Angeles, and Edward O. Orpet of Santa Barbara. Locally, Reichel made friends with members of the California Horticultural Society, attended their meetings in San

Francisco, and enlisted their help. Through these efforts, he was able to learn enough to combat the difficult growing conditions on Alcatraz.

Native California plants—which, he commented, were "more famous in England than here. It is so good to have plants which literally smile back at you."—were his first selections. His plantings of the native, white-flowered bush poppy (*Carpenteria californica*) and the brilliant, yellow-flowered flannel bush (*Fremontodendron californicum*) are no longer there, but his logic in choosing them demonstrated good horticultural sense.

He sought tough plants that could thrive on neglect or "even downright abuse." One of his most popular introductions was the showy, blue-flowered Pride of Madeira (*Echium fastuosum*). Since Reichel's time, a single plant acquired from Los Angeles nurseryman Hugh Evans has naturalized and the flowers of its now-mature seedlings still grace the island in early spring.

Probably on the advice of Ms. Sessions, who created the spectacular succulent gardens at San Diego's Balboa Park, he incorporated many succulents—aeonium, aloe, and sedum—in addition to ice plants and century plants. Bulbs, many of which come from the Mediterranean region and South Africa, were well-adapted to the island's wet winters and dry summers and were also on Reichel's list of favorites. He not only planted gladiolus, narcis-

LEFT: PRIDE OF MADEIRA *(Echium fastuosum)*

OPPOSITE: INMATE GARDENER ELLIOTT MICHENER IN FRONT OF WARDEN'S GREENHOUSE, CIRCA 1948

sus, and watsonia, but also experimented with hybridizing new varieties.

In time, Reichel cajoled his superiors into assigning trustees (inmate gardeners) to assist him, and willingly and patiently shared his passion for plants with them. At a time when prison officials gave no thought to rehabilitative therapies such as horticulture, Freddie Reichel must have been a positive influence on the inmates who helped him. He wrote of one man's amazement "to find that plants 'were like that' when I explained to him the mysteries of hybridization."

Success in beautifying the slope below the recreation yard tempted other inmate laborers, who often took flowers to brighten their cells. According to Reichel, "this meant sacrificing the use of the drinking glass and [tolerating] the sneers of their more stolid peers."

Returning for a visit years later, Reichel discovered to his delight and great pride that "the west lawn man [probably Elliott Michener or his friend Jack Giles] had been promoted . . . to the greenhouse and had branched out and cultivated and planted every place within sight of the officer on the roof. He was immensely proud of the results of his efforts," and showed Reichel where he had hidden his treasured hybridized narcissus, "for it seemed that other residents thought they were too pretty to stay in the gardens."

Another gardener from whom we have extensive information was Elliott Michener, who arrived as a prisoner on Alcatraz in 1941. He was assigned the weekend duty of retrieving softballs that went over the wall of the recreation yard onto the slope below, and helping to maintain the ice plant on

the same rather ragged incline. By December, he was working full-time, seven days a week, as the gardener for the area east of the fence dividing the slope. This was the beginning of a seven-year endeavor to create his garden. Years later, Michener described what this involved.

> My gardening work began with planting the strip of hill beside the steps with mesembryanthemum, so that all of the hillside would be the same—pink, laced with [yellow] oxalis. The terrace—six to ten feet wide on either side of a curbed, graveled road—had been gardened, apparently, for many years, but under difficulties. Nowhere was the soil more than four or five inches deep. Under that was solid yellow hardpan.
>
> I undertook what turned out to be a two-year task: breaking up the hardpan to a depth of two-and-a-half feet, screening it, fertilizing it with thousands upon thousands of five-gallon pails of garbage lugged up from the incinerator and disposal area. . . . As the garbage rotted and the beds subsided, I planted them with Iceland poppies, stock, and snapdragon, all supplied by my friend Dick Franseen. Later, I got permission from Warden Johnston to send out for seeds and plants and was able to raise picture-beds of delphinium, chrysanthemum, dahlias, and iris. . . . All the water for the hillside and the terrace came from the general supply, brought in by barge. There was never any attempt to conserve on it.
>
> A life-long friend . . . Richard C. Franseen, AZ-387, gardened on the other side of the island. He had a very small greenhouse and a small garden, which I never saw. Dick was a happy-go-lucky farm boy who had a good knowledge of how to grow plants.

Franseen gave Michener seed catalogs to study as well as provided him with seeds and plants propagated in his greenhouse. Michener was also befriended by a tough but compassionate guard, Captain Weinhold, who helped him secure resources necessary for his garden—old windows that had been removed from the cellhouse and stored in the model shop were used to build a flimsy but serviceable greenhouse on the foundation of an earlier one. Weinhold also obtained plants and seeds for him on his trips to San Francisco. One day, after seeing the blisters on Michener's hands, he gave him a pair of gloves.

MINDY MANVILLE

WESTSIDE GARDENS TODAY

Michener's labor converted a barren terrace into a garden bursting with flowers: Shasta daisies, Iceland poppies, red-hot pokers, and many others. It was hard, tedious work, but he relished it as an escape from the stress of prison life.

As Michener's garden flourished, he provided large bouquets for the warden's house. In return, the warden's wife showed her appreciation by giving him seeds and plants. "During the last two years of my stay on the island, I worked as a houseboy and also cook for Warden Swope [who followed Warden Johnston] and his wife, and spent all my free time gardening. She raised tuberous begonias in a little greenhouse I built, and supplied whatever plants I wanted." This job lasted until he was released from Alcatraz in 1950.

A RICH TAPESTRY

Today, thanks in large part to these gardeners and their interests, there are over 145 species or varieties of plants in 105 known genera living on Alcatraz. This is a significant botanical achievement considering the fact that virtually all these plants were introduced to the island, some over a century ago, and have survived the rigorous environment and more than thirty years of neglect.

Choices made by the island's various gardeners and by "beautification" leaders reflect a variety of human needs and plant preferences over a century and a half. No doubt some of the varieties planted were fortuitous selections that survived as lucky immigrants, while others met their demise from too much wind or drought or both. However, the plants that thrive on the island today have done so in part because they found their niches and energetically filled them. In a real sense, they form new communities as they compete for space, die, and regenerate. In turn, they create new habitats for other plants and for wildlife, especially birds.

In the 1870s, Victorian-era garden, preferences were for a great variety of showy exotic plants. Institutional requirements mandated plants appropriate for erosion control—ice plant and honeysuckle—and windbreaks, such as cypress and eucalyptus. "Beautification" brought wildflowers (poppies and lupine), nasturtiums, and trees (pines, and redwoods that ultimately failed to thrive). The gardeners also indulged their personal plant interests: Freddie Reichel sought out rare plants; officers and prison staff and their families tended toward roses and fuchsias; bulbs and brightly flowering plants were often favored by the inmate gardeners.

CALIFORNIA POPPY (*Eschscholzia californica*)

Each rationale for planting introduced yet another botanical variation into a place where no one would ordinarily have considered planting anything at all. As a composite, these individual choices created an island garden that has evolved over the years into a rich tapestry.

Today, the plants of Alcatraz include favorites of earlier periods. Some date back to the late 1800s while others are from the mid-twentieth century. Some have faded from favor while others, such as many of the bulbs, seem timeless. Most of the island's roses are now found only in specialty nurseries or are no longer propagated, having been replaced by newer, showier types. Following is a discussion of Alcatraz's plants, all of which represent groups historically favored by California gardeners (see map on pages 68 and 69 for general site locations).

ROSES

No doubt the favorite plant on Alcatraz is also one of the most cherished of the ages, the rose, whose flower is a symbol of enduring love. Though individual varieties may seem delicate, the family includes some of the world's most resilient plants.

On Alcatraz, we find cascading banks of rambling roses tumbling down the rocky slopes, climbers scrambling into trees and onto fences, and shrub roses used for hedging or for cut flowers. The dates when the various roses were introduced in nurseries provide clues as to when they might have been planted on Alcatraz: nineteenth-century roses by the military, twentieth-century roses during the federal Prison Bureau period.

Alcatraz's roses can be found in two main areas. One of these is near the foundation of an old greenhouse on the terrace south of the recreation yard, where we find the most hardy of the rambler roses: 'Russeliana,' 'Dorothy Perkins,' 'Excelsa,' and 'Félicité et Pérpetue.' The other is documented in photographs showing roses at the warden's house. The types of roses found there today are more refined than the south terrace's rugged ramblers and include 'General MacArthur,' 'Blaze,' 'Gardenia,' and 'Gloire des Rosomanes,' all of which are suitable for residential gardens.

The toughest and best-adapted roses, a strain of ramblers from eastern Asia (where they can often be found growing at the edge of the sea), *Rosa wichuraiana* and its many varieties are well-suited to the rigors of Alcatraz's marine climate. Blooming only once in the spring, wichuraiana's masses of bloom are unexcelled. The following varieties can be found today (dates in parentheses indicate year of nursery introduction): 'Gardenia' (1899), a graceful plant that grows to twenty feet high and has sprays of yellow to creamy white, apple-scented flowers; 'Dorothy Perkins' (1901), a climber or rambler with

ABOVE: *Rosa* 'EXCELSA'
OPPOSITE: *Rosa* 'GENERAL MACARTHUR'

Rosa 'FÉLICITÉ ET PÉRPETUE'

masses of small pink flowers; and 'Excelsa' (1909), sometimes called 'Red Dorothy Perkins,' a prostrate rambler with large clusters of small, double, crimson flowers.

Several other sprawling roses can be found tumbling over the rocky slopes of the island. One is an old favorite and the other a popular twentieth-century variety. 'Félicité et Pérpetue' (1827), is an evergreen (Sempervirens class) rambler, providing good ground cover for slopes, with small, white, double flowers in large clusters. 'Blaze' (1932), a hybrid of the popular 'Paul's Scarlet Climber,' is also a climber or trailer with very showy, slightly fragrant, brilliant scarlet, semi-double flowers in large clusters.

Below the warden's house is an early hybrid tea rose, 'General MacArthur' (1905). The namesake of this rose, General Arthur MacArthur, father of Douglas, had direct ties to Alcatraz. Around 1900, as a U.S. Army departmental commander, he was responsible for Alcatraz and other San Francisco Bay forts. No longer in production, 'General MacArthur' was a favorite during the early decades of this century, both as a garden hybrid tea and as a greenhouse rose. Its flowers are semi-double, rather open, very fragrant, and "military in color" according to MacFarland in *Modern Roses IV.* Although it was among the top ten roses of 1917, not all rose fanciers agreed with its position, as revealed by the acerbic comment of Jack Harkness in *Roses:* "A good constitution is a great help to a rose, and so is a memorable name. Those two assets must have helped 'General MacArthur' to its forty years in favour, because it was not a remarkable rose in other respects. The colour is cherry red, the flowers are thin, open quickly, and possess no great charm in form. But it was healthy, it grew well, and flowered freely."

GERANIUMS AND PELARGONIUMS

Another staple of California gardens, geraniums and pelargoniums ('Lady Washington' geraniums) are found in many places on Alcatraz. Their planting probably dates to the army period, both as garden plants in the officers' gardens and for beautification efforts in the early 1900s. Most of these, such as 'Alphonse Ricard' and 'Prince Bismarck,' are found on the island's more protected leeward side, near the sally port.

Federal penitentiary-era gardeners were most likely responsible for the plants found on the windward side below the cellhouse and the recreation yard. Despite drought, wind, and neglect, these plants are surprisingly healthy. The ease of propagating pelargoniums and geraniums from cuttings helps explain their abundance on the island.

Some of the more common pelargonium varieties found today include the 'California Brilliant,' with small, single, deep-magenta flowers, found in the greenhouse garden; 'Prince Bismarck,' with its single lavender flowers, found everywhere on the island; 'Alphonse Ricard,' a bright-red double-flowered geranium originally from France, popular in early twentieth-century California gardens and found throughout Alcatraz; and 'San Antonio,' a compact shrub with showy white-and-pink-blotched flowers, popular in California gardens in the 1930s—one shrub remains at the top of the stairs on the west side of the recreation yard.

FUCHSIAS

Long signature plants in California's coastal gardens, hybrid fuchsias have endured the rigors of Alcatraz surprisingly well. Originally from tropical Central and South America, they require cool, moist air; ample soil moisture; and protection from wind and hot sun. The fuchsias that remain on Alcatraz have survived on winter rain and summer fog. A recent pest, the fuchsia mite, has deformed the leaves of some of the plants, but most seem fairly healthy, though overgrown and neglected.

PELARGONIUM 'PRINCE BISMARCK'

The Alcatraz varieties include Firecracker Fuchsia (*Fuchsia magellanica*), the hardiest of all fuchsias and the parent of most hybrids—this dainty, red-and-purple-flowered shrub from the Magellan Mountains of southern Chile is found in the warden's garden; 'Riccarton' (*Fuchsia magellanica riccartonii*), whose origin in the garden at Riccarton near Edinburgh, Scotland, in the 1830s attests to its hardiness, has delicate, single flowers with long, narrow, recurved, scarlet sepals and purple corollas, reminiscent of a ballerina in costume; 'Mrs. Lovell Swisher,' introduced in 1942, has single flowers with pinkish-white sepals and deep rosy corollas—a vigorous example is found near the sally port; and 'Rose of Castile,' an old variety that has been a staple of gardens since its introduction in the mid-1800s— this shrubby plant produces large, single flowers with pale blush-pink sepals and purple corollas and is the most common fuchsia on the island, found near the electric shop and in the greenhouse garden below the recreation yard.

BULBS AND BULBLIKE PLANTS

Among the world's most popular garden plants, bulbs and bulblike plants are eminently well-suited to Alcatraz's climate. In fact, many of our common bulbs (daffodils, tulips, grape hyacinths, and gladiolus) originated in arid Mediterranean-type regions, principally the Mediterranean Basin and South Africa. All of the plants from these regions found a home so similar to their original habitat that they have naturalized on Alcatraz. In fact, a few have exerted themselves into the category of weeds, crowding out other plants.

Their design for survival is perfectly suited to the San Francisco Bay Area's long, dry summers and cool, rainy winters. The whole plant is literally a subterranean package that remains dormant during the summer and autumn. With winter rains, it springs to life, first producing leaves and later spectacular bursts of flowers. Some bulbs expend their blooms in a few weeks while others continue their show until the soil dries out. The

'RICCARTON'(*Fuchsia magellanica riccartonii*)

DOUGLAS IRIS *(Iris douglasiana)*

straplike leaves of most bulbs function to catch any available moisture, even fog or dew, and funnel it to the bulb and its roots—an ingenious design for arid climates.

A visitor to the Rock in early spring is likely to find a colorful show put on by the following plants, arranged by region of origin.

MEDITERRANEAN BASIN: Spanish bluebell (*Endymion hispanicus*), bulb; lilac-flowered iris (*Iris spuria*), rhizome; snowflake (*Leucojum aestivum*), bulb, white nodding flowers with green tips; grape hyacinth (*Muscari armeniacum*), bulb, purple grape-like flower spikes; narcissus (*Narcissus* spp.), bulb, several types, including winter-blooming, fragrant paperwhites; tulip (*Tulipa* spp.), bulb, several hybrids of varying colors.

SOUTH AFRICA: Naked Lady (*Amaryllis belladonna*), bulb, clusters of summer blooming bright pink trumpet flowers on long leafless stalks; chasmanthe (*Chasmanthe floribunda*), corm, red-orange flowers on tall spikes; gladiolus (*Gladiolus* spp.), corm, several varieties with different colors; Bermuda buttercup (*Oxalis pes-caprae*), bulb, clear yellow flowers with clover-like leaves; watsonia (*Watsonia* spp.), corm, several species and varieties ranging from purple-pink to brilliant orange flowers on tall spikes (similar to chasmanthe in growth).

CALIFORNIA: Douglas iris (*Iris douglasiana*), rhizome, low, blue-flowered iris, native to the coast; Ithuriel's Spear (*Triteleia laxa, Brodiaea* var.), corm, clusters of purple-blue trumpets on a tall stalk, native to the coast and interior of California.

UNIQUE PLANTS

Alcatraz seems an unlikely place to find unusual or rare plants. Yet, amidst the common roses, geraniums, and fuchsias, we find about a dozen plants today considered to be unique or rare due to their general absence in mainland gardens and other landscape plantings—they are most likely to be found in botanical garden collections or the gardens of avid horticulturists. They were discovered in a 1992 inventory of the island's plants; all are well-adapted to the harsh conditions of the island and to neglect. Such rigorous testing may warrant their "re-discovery" and use in California's landscape plantings and coastal gardens. Descriptions of six of the specimens follow.

As visitors arrive at the dock eager to learn about the intrigue of the prison, they pass by a rugged old shrub very much at home on the island: *Athanasia parviflora*, a member of the Compositae (daisy) family from South Africa. This large shrub bulges out above the amphitheater constructed below the steep slope to the south of Building 64. Its leaves are so deeply divided or segmented that one might mistake it for a conifer. In late spring, its three- to four-inch-in-diameter, dense and rounded yellow flower heads bring this otherwise undistinguished shrub to life—the intense sulfur-yellow flowers resemble the common yarrow. After blooming, it fades into the background, unnoticed but content in its protected island niche.

Agave lecheguilla is related to the century plant (*A. americana*) but is smaller, a two-foot-tall plant native to Texas and northern Mexico. Other than its location on the southwest side of the island, this rare succulent is found only at the University of California Berkeley Botanical Garden and in a private succulent garden.

Echium pininana is similar to the common Pride of Madeira (*E. fastuosum*) but has taller spikes of deep blue flowers that create a dramatic display in early spring. Both are from the Canary Islands.

Olearia traversii is a large evergreen shrub native to New Zealand. Quite common there, it is rarely found in the Bay Area.

Two unusual and previously unknown species of watsonia, the striking, purple-pink flowered bulblike plant mentioned earlier, were also found during the 1992 plant inventory. One has a soft orange, tubular flower and the other, a brilliant orange, flared, trumpet-like flower. All watsonias are from South Africa.

Agave lecheguilla

ABOVE: PLUME ALBIZIA LEAVES *(Albizia distachya)*
OPPOSITE: SYDNEY GOLDEN WATTLE LEAVES *(Acacia longifolia)*

SEASIDE PLANTS

The island's gardens are a unique testing ground for seaside plants. Those that have endured have a number of traits in common, including origination in Mediterranean-type climatic regions; adaptation to cool summers and mild winters free of frost; toleration of strong, frequently salt-laden winds and fog and poor, rocky, or shallow soils; and the ability to survive on winter rainfall and summer fog.

Following are the seaside plants that are now growing on the island; some are also California natives.

TREES: Monterey cypress (*Cupressus macrocarpa*), red gum (*Eucalyptus camaldulensis*), common fig (*Ficus carica*), Australian tea tree (*Leptospermum laevigatum*), New Zealand Christmas tree (*Metrosideros excelsus*).

SHRUBS: Sydney golden wattle (*Acacia longifolia*), plume albizia (*Albizia distachya*), *Athanasia parviflora*, rockrose (*Cistus hybridus*), mirror plant (*Coprosma repens*), Pride of Madeira (*Echium candicans, E. fastuosum*), Veronica Lake (*Hebe* spp.), tree mallow (*Lavatera arborea*), malva rosa (*L. assurgentiflora*), firethorn (*Pyracantha coccinea*), coffeeberry (*Rhamnus californica*), *Rosa wichuraiana* and varieties, California fuchsia (*Zauschneria californica, Z. cana*).

SUCCULENTS: Aeonium (*Aeonium arboreum*), century plant (*Agave americana*), torch plant (*Aloe arborescens*), Hottentot fig (*Carpobrotus edulis*), pink ice plant (*Drosanthemum floribunda*), green cockscomb (*Sedum dendroideum praealtum*), Spanish bayonet (*Yucca aloifolia*), Spanish dagger (*Y. gloriosa*).

ANNUALS: Red valerian (*Centranthus ruber*), California poppy (*Eschscholzia californica*), garden nasturtium (*Tropaeoleum majus*).

CALIFORNIA NATIVE PLANTS

Few California native plants can be found on Alcatraz today—the 1992 inventory recorded only twelve commonly cultivated woody and herbaceous native species. Though surprising, this is not unusual, as traditional gardening in the late nineteenth and early twentieth century emphasized exotic plants, a preference that persists in many contemporary gardens and landscapes.

In 1983, a group of volunteers under the direction of Robert C. Crabb planted endangered California native plants on the island. Of the thirty-one species listed in a January 1984 memo from Crabb, only four can be found today. One would have hoped for more survivors.

Those native plants that still "smile back at you" on the island include: Monterey cypress, tree mallow, California coffeeberry, California fuchsia, Douglas iris, bush lupine (*Lupinus arboreus*), checker mallow (*Sidalcea malvaeflora*), California polypody fern (*Polypodium californicum*), leather leaf fern (*P. scouleri*), Western sword fern (*Polystichum munitum*), Ithuriel's Spear, and California poppy.

FRUIT TREES

Because fruit trees usually demand more care and a warmer climate than is found on Alcatraz, it is surprising to see them here. But here they are, in the greenhouse garden area below the recreation yard—an apple, a peach, a walnut, and several fig trees. Beneath the latter is a ruin of a bird bath that Elliott Michener designed and built in the 1940s. He recalls that the trees were fairly large when he began work in this garden around 1942. They were probably planted in the mid- to late 1930s, during the federal prison period, possibly by Freddie Reichel or his gardeners.

ABOVE: AUSTRALIAN TEA TREE *(Leptospermum laevigatum)*
OPPOSITE: CALIFORNIA POLYPODY FERN *(Polypodium californicum)*

NIGHTSHADE *(Solanum americanum)* FRUIT

THE INVADERS

Weedy plants often accompany humans—sometimes accidentally, in the form of seeds caught on fabric, wheels, or in mud on shoes or tools. Others are intentionally introduced by gardeners unaware of the plant's invasive nature. On Alcatraz, seven of these "escaped exotics" are considered noxious weeds and have become both widespread and well-established. They out-compete other plants for the scarce water and limited soil resources, or simply smother smaller varieties. It is reasonable to assume that the colonization of the island by this "gang of seven" will continue and many more ornamental plants will be eradicated as time goes on unless an effort is made to control these noxious colonizers from the main garden areas—the greenhouse, the warden's house and officers' row foundations, the south terraces, the sally port, and the area beneath the water tank.

These invaders include pampas grass *(Cortaderia jubata)*, an extremely aggressive specimen that has spread by wind-blown seeds throughout coastal California; false garlic *(Nothoscordum gracile)*, a bulbous plant that colonizes large areas and crowds out smaller plants; Bermuda buttercup, another bulbous plant with attractive yellow flowers; wild radish *(Raphanus sativus)*, a two- to three-foot-tall plant that reseeds prolifically, colonizing large areas and crowding and shading smaller plants; blackberry *(Rubus* spp.), the worst of which is the Himalayan blackberry *(R. discolor)*, which colonizes and smothers all but the tallest trees with an impenetrable thorny bramble; German ivy *(Senecio mikanioides)*, a deceivingly delicate plant that has colonized many of the shady areas on the island's eastern section; and finally, nightshade *(Solanum americanum)*, a highly poisonous plant that colonizes areas that have been disturbed.

THE TRUE MEANING OF GARDENS

Aesthetically, Alcatraz's plantings lack a designer's approach to composition, color, texture, form, and space. But in winter and spring, as though gracing an ancient ruin, their great beauty emerges in a kaleidoscope of color. The old rambling roses, the pink ice plant, and the geraniums contribute beauty to this stern place.

When we realize the extraordinary effort that was required to create that beauty, aesthetic appreciation becomes visceral. Suddenly we appreciate the true meaning of the gardens: the human drama they represent.

They are transformed from simple, lovely artifacts of the past to part of a dynamic process that changed the lives of the gardeners, who invested not only their energies but also their spirits.

Familiar stories of life inside the prison abound—human despair and suffering, brutality and deception, failure. Outside the cells, however, the stories of the gardeners and their gardens speak of release, creativity, joy, and success. Many who gardened on Alcatraz may have been changed by the process. For Freddie Reichel it became a passion, nearly an obsession. His work in the gardens not only helped him endure the stress of helping administer this most fearsome of prisons, but also unleashed a previously untapped creativity. In the process of nurturing and studying plants and sharing that passion with his inmate gardeners, he became an excellent horticulturist, a hobby he enjoyed the rest of his life.

Elliott Michener found freedom in his gardens. "The hillside provided a refuge from disturbances of the prison, the work a release, and it became an obsession. This one thing I would do well. . . . If we are all our own jailers, and prisoners of our traits, then I am grateful for my introduction to the spade and trowel, the seed and the spray can. They have given me a lasting interest in creativity. At eighty-nine, I'm still at it." One can only

ABOVE: THE WARDEN'S HOUSE ROSE GARDEN TODAY
OPPOSITE: FIRETHORN *(Pyracantha coccinea)* BERRIES

imagine—and hope—that others had their spirits lifted and their lives changed in the same way: families of military men and Prison Bureau employees; military prisoners in the army's vocational program; the unknown men tutored by Freddie Reichel; Robinson, who preceded Michener; Dick Franseen and Jack Giles, Michener's friends; and those for whom there is no recorded information.

Charles Lewis, champion of horticulture as therapy, succinctly sums the real lesson of gardening:

> *From a human perspective, the strength of gardening lies in nurturing. Caring for another living entity is a basic quality of being human. Plants are alive and dependent on the gardener for care if they are to survive. In a world of constant judgment, plants are non-threatening and non-discriminating. They respond to the care given to them, not to the race or the intellectual or physical capacities of the gardener. . . . Plants take away some of the anxiety and tension of the immediate NOW by showing us that there are long, enduring patterns in life.*

Paradise Reclaimed

A NEW PERSPECTIVE ON THE GARDENS OF ALCATRAZ

ABOVE: PRIDE OF MADEIRA *(Echium fastuosum)*
PREVIOUS: CENTURY PLANT *(Agave americana)*

Paradise Reclaimed

A NEW PERSPECTIVE ON THE GARDENS OF ALCATRAZ

—

MICHAEL BOLAND

"Garden" is a familiar word, evoking images of carefully tended personal patches of paradise. Few would associate the idea of garden with Alcatraz—fewer still would associate "paradise," that oldest and most universal of garden metaphors, with the island's derelict penitentiary landscape. Yet in many ways, Alcatraz is a paradise reclaimed, a landscape where a balance has been struck once again between human invention and natural vitality. The gardens of Alcatraz are the result of an ongoing recombination of apparent opposites—nature and culture—into a string of gardens that are neither entirely natural nor entirely human-made, but rather, a synthesis of both.

On Alcatraz, there is a suggestion that humans and wildlife can coexist if a more flexible attitude about the boundary between nature and culture is developed. It demonstrates that the broader environment can accommodate people and wildlife most effectively in a finely intermeshed series of habitats.

Modern Alcatraz bears little resemblance to the pre-settlement hump-backed, barren island described in 1849 by 49'er Hiram Pierce as looking like "a great snow-bank . . . perfectly white with guano." The contemporary landscape reflects a spectrum of everyday decisions and activities

WESTERN GULLS IN RUBBLE PILE

intended to adapt the island to new uses. Over the last century and a half, these dramatic changes have obliterated and then remade the primordial richness of scrubby, guano-covered "Bird Island."

A close look at the landscape of Alcatraz, however, reveals that *la Isla des los Alcatraces* has not vanished under concrete and asphalt, but has been remade by it. The careful observer finds an island teeming with wildlife occupying a created landscape, a unique amalgam of human history and natural process.

Early Americans saw Alcatraz as both a hazard to navigation and as an opportunity to protect the strategically significant entrance to San Francisco Bay. Thus began the process of landscape transformation: massive grading and excavation to shape roadways, support building foundations and terraced gardens, and carve gun batteries from the rock; building recycling and reconstruction to accommodate ever-evolving needs and uses; and planting for general beautification of the island and to serve the various human communities that called Alcatraz their home.

Another group also called Alcatraz home, and with the closure of the penitentiary in 1963, a process of recolonization by wildlife began. The arrival of birds such as western gulls, pigeon guillemots, and pelagic cormorants marked a re-inhabitation, as they quite likely nested on Alcatraz prior to the dramatic landscape manipulations of the 1850s. Generally, they have chosen to colonize those sections of the island most like primordial Alcatraz, particularly the rugged and barren western cliffs. Other nesting sites are also popular; many of these are entirely developed, such as the paved concrete parade ground.

New avian arrivals on the island include Anna's hummingbirds, mallards, and black-crowned night herons, birds not previously seen on Alcatraz. In some cases, these colonies have grown to numbers significant in the context of San Francisco Bay—for example, the black-crowned night heron colony on Alcatraz has grown to 15 percent of the total Bay Area heron population. This can be linked directly to human actions, specifically, the creation of gardens on Alcatraz.

THE GARDENS THROUGH A DIFFERENT LENS

Some of the island's gardens are defined by fences and sturdy concrete borders. However, it is possible to look at them through a different lens, one in which biological value is weighted as heavily as scenic beauty. Considered in this way, the gardens of Alcatraz are delineated neither by borders nor clipped hedges but rather by invisible lines that separate the domains in which natural processes have, by default, been allowed to proceed unencumbered. These gardens are no longer simply a utilitarian collection of plants grouped for effect. They have quite unexpectedly given rise to something more akin to a single organism—a living assemblage of plants and wildlife.

The island and its gardens are proof that wildlife habitat can be important without being pristine wilderness, that a great egret nesting in a non-native eucalyptus tree or a western gull nesting in a rubble pile is not a citizen of a second-class wild kingdom. In fact, these gardens suggest that nature is a resilient and mischievous set of relationships and processes, not so very worried about how a thing looks but rather how it functions, how its habitats are structured, and what needs it fulfills for its inhabitants.

Alcatraz offers itself as a compact field laboratory for the examination of some of these relationships and functions. In its essentially three basic types of "gardens" or habitats (ornamental, primordial, and constructed) the visitor can see a range of natural and human processes at work. A trip through the gardens of Alcatraz is a journey through time and nature, and well worth taking.

ABOVE: VINES FRAME A RUSTING HYDRANT
OPPOSITE: PINK ESCALLONIA

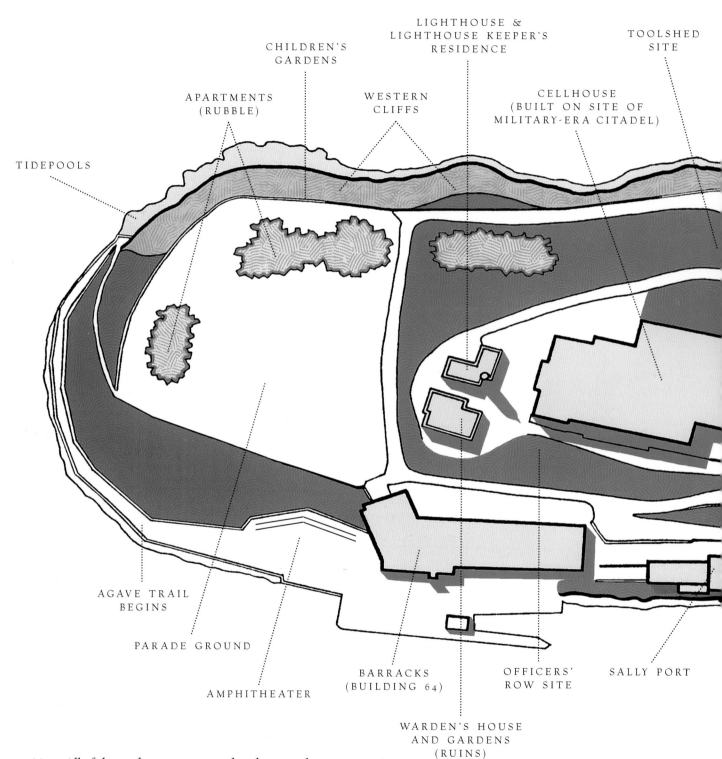

TIDEPOOLS

APARTMENTS
(RUBBLE)

CHILDREN'S
GARDENS

WESTERN
CLIFFS

LIGHTHOUSE &
LIGHTHOUSE KEEPER'S
RESIDENCE

TOOLSHED
SITE

CELLHOUSE
(BUILT ON SITE OF
MILITARY-ERA CITADEL)

AGAVE TRAIL
BEGINS

PARADE GROUND

AMPHITHEATER

BARRACKS
(BUILDING 64)

OFFICERS'
ROW SITE

SALLY PORT

WARDEN'S HOUSE
AND GARDENS
(RUINS)

*Note: All of the gardens are associated with particular structures (not
all of which still exist) or with specific locations.*

68

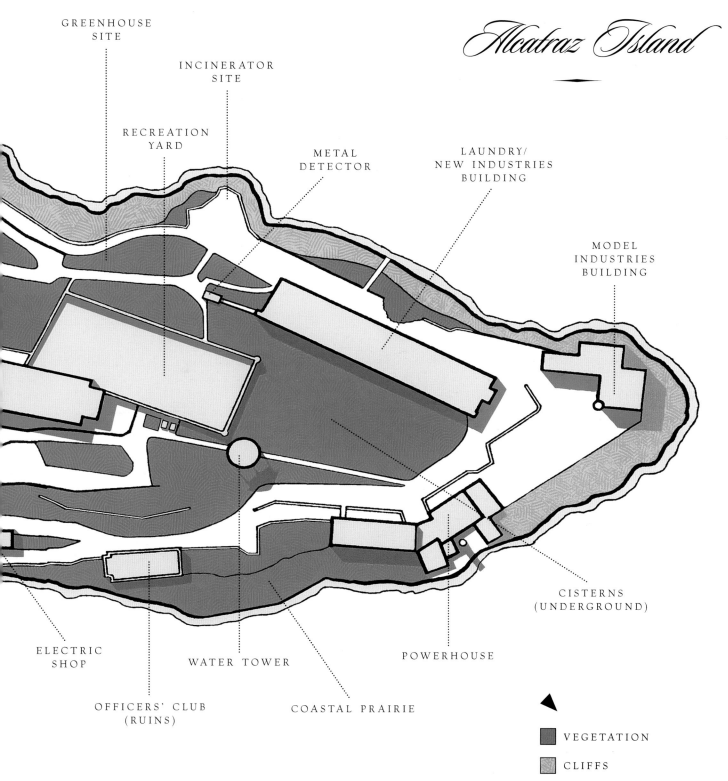

GREENHOUSE
SITE

INCINERATOR
SITE

RECREATION
YARD

METAL
DETECTOR

LAUNDRY/
NEW INDUSTRIES
BUILDING

MODEL
INDUSTRIES
BUILDING

Alcatraz Island

CISTERNS
(UNDERGROUND)

ELECTRIC
SHOP

WATER TOWER

POWERHOUSE

OFFICERS' CLUB
(RUINS)

COASTAL PRAIRIE

VEGETATION

CLIFFS

69

ORNAMENTAL GARDENS

An ornamental garden is one that is created for pleasure, and on
Alcatraz, the tradition is nearly as old as permanent human habitation.
By 1853, soil brought from Angel Island and the mainland had been
used to create a series of terraced gardens near the citadel. With this
soil came the seeds of many native plants that may be seen on Alcatraz
today as well as other likely stowaways; genetic analysis of the slender
salamanders that inhabit the islands of the bay show a similarity
between those on Angel Island and on Alcatraz.

A simple square of closely cropped turf, tidy rows of potted geraniums and century plants along narrow roadways, and the small cottage
garden adjacent to the brick citadel mark the start of a tradition of gardening that has ebbed and flowed on Alcatraz for the more than a century. Subsequent efforts, driven by both functional and beautification
needs, diversified the structure and variety of the once uniformly barren
landscape. Invasive vines such as Japanese honeysuckle, spreading
hybrids of *Rosa wichuraiana*, and ice plant were planted on the many
slopes disturbed by grading. In an effort to soften the "prison island's"
profile, trees were brought to the island, mostly Monterey cypress,
Australian tea trees, and various eucalyptus. As part of this same effort,
extensive shrubby borders of nineteenth- and early twentieth-century
rose hybrids, mirror bush, and flowering perennial species numerous
and varied were also added.

Since 1963, the gardens have been left to their own devices and have
grown with unbridled vigor into a melange, each uniquely constituted.
The end result is a landscape far more complex in structure and varied
in habitat than the original Alcatraz. The island's main paths string this
unique collection of gardens together.

JAPANESE HONEYSUCKLE *(Lonicera japonica)* WITH BLACKBERRY *(Rubus wisinus)*

ABOVE: NARCISSUS IN THE SALLY PORT GARDEN
OPPOSITE: HEBE

SALLY PORT GARDEN

Disembarking from the ferry and proceeding up the main road to the cellhouse, you quickly encounter the first ornamental garden, associated with the old brick sally port. The sally port, or guardhouse, protected the entrance to fortress Alcatraz. The plantings in this garden coincide with late nineteenth-century efforts to beautify the military prison grounds. In early spring, clumps of sweet-scented narcissus bloom beneath the gnarled Australian tea trees, dragon trees (*Dracaena draco*), and time-ravaged fuchsias. Early summer brings the towering white spires of watsonia and delicate clusters of palest pink roses, the early nineteenth-century hybrid 'Félicité et Pérpetue.'

The gardens continue on the far side of the sally port. Beyond the burned-out shell of the officers' club, the steep hillsides are densely covered with species whose function is to hold the hillside in place, such as English ivy, pale lavender drosanthemum, Japanese honeysuckle, and hebe. The steepest slopes are confined by elaborate retaining walls, often built of recycled concrete or granite blocks. Cliff-dwelling colonists such as the California polypody fern and red valerian have found a home in the walls' damp crevices. These "erosion control" gardens represent the first use of ornamental plantings on Alcatraz.

Passing the parade ground at the second bend in the road and proceeding to the third, you encounter another of the handful of native species to be found on Alcatraz, a sprawling coffeeberry plant. More typically found in moist coastal scrub or semi-shady woodland conditions, the coffeeberry is named for the resemblance its glossy green leaves and choco-late-brown fruits bear to *Coffee arabica*, the com-mercial coffee plant.

WATER TOWER GARDEN

From this small native patch, your eye is next drawn to the looming water tower and the small garden patch at its base. This area between the water tower and the main path was the site of the first housing on Alcatraz, built during the 1850s. It continued to be used for housing by non-commissioned officers into the 1940s. The plants here were undoubtedly associated with this housing, and most likely represent the oldest strictly ornamental plantings on the island. Springtime in the water tower garden brings the yellow-orange of coastal California poppies and multi-hued purple Dutch iris, followed by watsonia's soft

orange spires. By mid-summer, golden grass sets off the bright crimson flowers of a rambling 'Dorothy Perkins' rose that has spread to fill most of the water tower garden with its richly hued and plentiful single blooms.

OFFICERS' ROW GARDEN

Brick foundations are all that remain of officers' row. Once a string of fine Victorian houses with small formal garden terraces between them and planter boxes filled with geraniums and agave in front, these structures were demolished during the transformation of the island into a federal penitentiary. Thereafter, gardens were maintained among the brick foundations. Today, deep-red and purple firecracker fuchsias, pure white callas, English ivy, and red valerian bloom in the ruins.

WARDEN'S HOUSE GARDEN

At the end of officers' row stands what remains of the commandant's or warden's house. Prior to its burning, the seventeen-room house included a conservatory and several terraces with spectacular bay views that enhanced the warden's private garden. Subsequent erosion has

ABOVE: *Rosa* 'DOROTHY PERKINS'
OPPOSITE: OFFICER'S ROW, CIRCA 1902

destroyed much of the south terrace, although some plume albizia and agave (*Agave americana*) are still visible here. The east terrace remains largely intact, adorned by the large-flowered, fragrant black-red tea rose, 'General MacArthur'; a creamy-yellow rose hybrid, 'Gardenia'; and tiny deep-red and purple firecracker fuchsias. Loud orange nasturtiums and brilliant red valerian have turned the warden's house itself into a garden, carpeting the ground floor of the ruined residence all summer long.

GREENHOUSE GARDEN

Ornamental gardens on Alcatraz were largely limited to the eastern side of the island until the 1920s and 1930s. During these two decades, ornamental plantings were extended around the south and west side of Alcatraz. Today as you continue on the main road past the cellhouse, you reach the extensive terraced plantings of the greenhouse garden on the slopes below the west cellhouse wall. Looking at the current unkempt and overgrown condition of these gardens, it is difficult to imagine that they were once highly manicured, with tidy hedge-lined paths and two closely cropped lawns tended by inmates. As you pass beneath the large, dark green New Zealand Christmas tree, the upper gardens present themselves as a jumble of overgrown shrubs, including species like privet and cotoneaster usually shorn as hedges. A dense stand of blackberries on the left side of the path marks what was once a semi-circular expanse of lawn; from here, a spectacular view of the Golden Gate spreads out. Across the path, a scattering of plume albizia and scruffy weeds marks the extent of the

ABOVE: BUMBLEBEE IN PLUME ALBIZIA
OPPOSITE: AEONIUM HYBRID

larger rectangular lawn that was sustained by greywater from the cell-house that towers nearby.

Continuing along, you encounter a thicket of domestic figs and Japanese honeysuckle. From March to August, a strange, guttural clacking noise, the sounds of black-crowned night herons, emanates from this woody hedge. These birds have nested on Alcatraz since the mid-1970s, returning early each spring and remaining until late summer. Breeding season is indicated by the color of the birds themselves: their legs and feet, normally yellow, turn red, and the black on their head and back takes on a blue-green gloss. Black-crowned night herons nest in several colonies scattered around the island. All are in the dense, shrubby, non-native vegetation—mirror bush, Australian tea tree, and Sydney golden wattle—planted in the island's gardens. One of largest collection of herons' nests is here in the greenhouse garden. During breeding season, the gawky juvenile herons can often be seen flapping about, trying out their wings.

Beyond the toolshed, the gardens open up with a series of terraces spilling down the hillsides. For most of the year, a riot of color covers these slopes, a jumble of chrome-yellow aeoniums, magenta 'Prince Bismarck' pelargoniums, blue-violet Pride of Madeira, and single white roses. Several old roses are at home here, including the island's most fragrant, an old mauve hybrid, 'Russeliana.' Passing the foundations of the former greenhouse, a small grove of apple trees marks another set of terraces cascading downslope. A second jumble of roses, fuchsias, wayward artichokes, and agave tumbles down this slope to the incinerator site below. The greenhouse gardens terminate at the metal detector building, where an overgrown privet hedge obscures the narrow bridge that connects the gardens to the laundry building and the north end of the island.

ARTICHOKES IN SUMMER

THE GRASSLANDS

Dominating the skyline of Alcatraz are three structures: the cellhouse, the lighthouse, and a decrepit, welded-steel water tower. At the base of the water tower are the ruins of a previous attempt at water storage, two much-smaller concrete cisterns, built like their larger cousin to hold water shipped via barge from Sausalito.

On the rocky outcropping at the base of the water tower is one of the best preserved remnants of pre-settlement Alcatraz, a small coastal prairie. Green in springtime and golden by summer, this prairie goes through the seasons in tandem with the rugged Marin Headlands, which can be seen to the northwest. Protected from human activity by steep topography and high walls, here more than at any other location, Alcatraz in its wild state can be imagined.

Come February, the silence of this isolated site is pierced by the cries of western gulls marking nesting territories, forming new family pairs, and setting to work at the business of breeding and raising young. The relative isolation of the cisterns, abandoned with the closure of the prison, has encouraged one of the largest groups of western gulls on Alcatraz to recolonize this area. They seem to find the plateau, created by military construction efforts, to be an ideal replica of their former island clifftop habitat. Flourishing in its isolation, this colony accounts for roughly 15 percent of the total gull population on Alcatraz.

On the cooler east side of the island, on the steep slopes below the powerhouse, can be found another fragment of coastal prairie. Protected from wind and salt spray, this prairie is a more verdant green-grey collection of native grasses, primarily native wild rye (*Elymus triticoides*). This small prairie is also notable for its concentration of deer mice, the only mammal found on Alcatraz besides *Homo sapiens*. Deer mice, ubiquitous throughout North America in a variety of habitats, are nocturnal mammals that feed on insects, grains, and fruit. The mice on Alcatraz are buff color, a variation of

COASTAL PRAIRIE, LOOKING TOWARD POWERHOUSE AND ANGEL ISLAND

CENTURY PLANT *(Agave americana)*

the darker brown found in the rest of the Bay Area population. They have carved a dense colony of tunnels into the loose rubble slopes in the prairie between the officers' club and the powerhouse structures.

THE WESTERN CLIFFS

As earlier noted, Alcatraz originally had a more rounded shape, with slopes that rose gradually from the waters of the bay. Today, approaching the island, the visitor is struck by the dramatic cliffs along the island's western reaches. These cliffs are in part the work of nature and in part, of man.

The blasting of the cliffs did more than make Alcatraz easier for its human inhabitants to defend. It also added to the steep cliff habitat favored by many pelagic birds and made these areas even more difficult for humans to access. This created a comfortable year-round home for the often-skittish bird species that populate the cliffs today. As time has passed, a number of new species has arrived, returning the western cliffs to a semblance of Alcatraz prior to settlement: pigeon guillemots, black oystercatchers, Brandt's cormorants, double-crested cormorants, pelagic cormorants, and western gulls. In some instances, Alcatraz is the only occurrence of these species within the San Francisco Bay.

THE AGAVE TRAIL AND
PARADE GROUND "GARDENS"

One of the most beautiful and bizarre gardens on Alcatraz is open to the public for only a portion of the year. Completed in 1994, the Agave Trail was designed by noted landscape architect Lawrence Halprin to provide public access to the southern part of Alcatraz for the first time. This is the island's "wild side," bereft of structures and one of the few places that you can be near the level of the bay.

This portion of Alcatraz has seen particularly dramatic landscape transformations. In the mid-nineteenth century, the army cut away most of the southern end of the island to create a flat parade ground for military exercises. Some of the rubble was used to fill small coves along the southern shore. The remainder, dumped over the side of the island, created the loose talus slope and submerged debris that rings the island's southern margins. Sometime thereafter, the parade ground was paved and construction of the first military prison began. Later parade-ground structures, including three-story apartment buildings for the families of the federal penitentiary guards, were demolished by the General Services Administration in 1972; large rubble piles are all that remain.

The Agave Trail provides access to this landscape. This "garden" begins at the broad concrete steps that create an amphitheater at the dock; the shape mimics the stepped buttress designed by the army to hold the cliff above in place. Several interesting species find a home on this cliff, including cabbage-like succulent aeoniums, a bright-red flowering California fuchsia, and a very unusual South American member of the sunflower family, *Athanasia parviflora*. Dense plantings of Australian tea tree and Sydney golden wattle on the slopes above house a nesting colony of black-crowned night herons. (To protect this colony, the Agave Trail is closed while they are in residence.) Passing through the tall chainlink gate, beyond the picnic tables and out from under the messy blue gum eucalyptus, you round the corner and encounter a spectacular view of the San Francisco skyline. If you cast a glance uphill, you will have your first encounter with the trail's namesake, *Agave americana*, the most common of three agave species found on Alcatraz. The dramatic grey-green, sword-shaped

LEFT: FLOWER, *Aloe arborescens*
OPPOSITE: SEA ANEMONE

rosettes have created a solid mat along the entire south slope of the island, their graceful, 20-foot-tall flower stalks providing a frame for the trail's spectacular views of city and bay.

Glance over the edge of the railing and you will see another type of Alcatraz "garden": tidepools. Over time, the rubble dumped into the bay

during the 1850s has evolved into one of the richest collections of tidepools within the bay, and certainly the only human-made tidepool of any significance along the central coast. At low tide, you can see sea anemones, sea urchins, starfish, and various tidepool species as you stroll along the waterside Agave Trail. Western gulls and other pelagic birds trawl the shallow waters here for a meal,

similar in many ways to far-larger tidepool gatherings on the Pacific Coast.

Moving up toward the parade ground, the Agave Steps provide three belvederes, seating areas protected from the wind and designed to offer slightly different perspectives on the grand views beyond. Upon reaching the parade ground, you will be immediately struck by the disorganized piles of building fragments, rebar, window casements, and old refrigerators that ring the broad, flat concrete surface. Once, this area was the heart of a community, apartment buildings with tidy foundation plantings of pelargoniums, hydrangeas, and pittosporum and carefully manicured lawns. Along the perimeter road, small garden plots—tiny personal gardens—were assigned to the children who lived on Alcatraz, Now, only a few forlorn artichoke plants mark these children's gardens. Slowly, the foundation plantings that once framed the entrances to buildings on the parade ground have spread to engulf the piles, turning them into large, green, landscaped mounds and increasing their value as habitat. Soon, only faint traces of the material underneath the green mantle will remain.

The rubble piles embrace the parade ground as the apartments once did. They have new occupants today: deer mice, slender salamanders, black-crowned night herons, western gulls, and even burrowing owls call them home. The parade ground, its smooth concrete surface fractured with grass-filled cracks, provides ideal nesting habitat for the largest of the western gull colonies on Alcatraz. During the breeding season (which lasts from approximately January to August), this particular gull colony is best observed from the road below the cellhouse. By the end of August, the gulls are gone and the parade ground is quiet once again.

GARDENS AS METAPHOR

Alcatraz is a landscape that defies simple labels. For some a cultural landmark and others a wildlife habitat, its significance lies in being both, two things inextricably bound together. Alcatraz, in its contemporary disheveled, multi-valent splendor, represents the quintessential garden, that place where human actions and natural processes dance a delicate ballet, perhaps even the type of place from which the idea of "environmental stewardship" stems. In the idea of the garden itself is the key to breaking down a conceptual deadlock between nature and culture, between wilderness and cities. Perhaps in this middle ground, a new ethic can emerge, one that allows more complexity in the landscape and more varied manifestations of the life force that animates all things. Perhaps in fact, in the garden is the preservation of the earth.

Aptenia cordifolia

Plants of Alcatraz

Following is a selected list of plants found on Alcatraz in the 1992 survey, "The Historical Gardens of Alcatraz Island, a Research Report for the Golden Gate National Park Association," made by Lutsko Associates, San Francisco, California.

Most of the plants are, or at one time were, considered as ornamentals and used in domestic gardens. A few plants on the list, such as giant reed (*Arundo donax*) and pampas grass (*Cortaderia jubata*) are considered weeds today because of their invasive tendencies.

Plants are listed alphabetically by Latin name, and the common name is given when known. A question mark in parentheses indicates a tentative species identification.

Acacia longifolia,
  Sydney Golden Wattle
Acanthus mollis, Bear's Breech
Aeonium arboreum
Aeonium sp. and hybrids
Agapanthus orientalis,
  Lily of the Nile
Agave americana, Century Plant
Agave americana, variegated
Agave lecheguilla
Agave sp.
Albizia distachya, Plume Albizia
Aloe arborescens, Torch Plant
Aloe sladeniana (?)
Amaryllis belladonna, Naked Lady
Aptenia cordifolia, Ice Plant type
Arundo donax, Giant Reed
Athanasia parviflora

Baccharis pilularis spp., Coyote Brush
Brassaia geniculata, Mustard

Carpobrotus chilensis (?), Ice Plant type
Carpobrotus edulis, Hottontot Fig
Centranthus ruber, Red Valerian
Chasmanthe floribunda
Chrysanthemum frutescens,
  Marguerite daisy
Cistus x hybridus, Rockrose
Coprosma repens, Mirror Plant
Cordyline australis, Giant Dracaena

Cortaderia jubata, Pampas Grass
Cotoneaster pannosa
Crassula argentea, Jade Plant
Crataegus sp., Hawthorne
Cupressus macrocarpa,
  Monterey Cypress
Cymbalaria muralis, Kenilworth ivy
Cynara solymus, Globe Artichoke

Dichondra micrantha
Dracaena draco, Dragon Tree
Drosanthemum floribunda,
  Pink Ice Plant

Echium fastuosum,
  Pride of Madeira
Echium pininana
Elymus triticoides, Wild Rye Grass
Endymion hispanicus,
  Spanish Bluebell
Escallonia sp.
Eschscholzia californica,
  California Poppy
Eucalyptus camaldulensis, Red Gum
Eucalyptus globulus, Blue Gum
Eucalyptus sp.
Eucalyptus tereticornis,
  Forest Red Gum
Euonymus japonica,
  Evergreen Euonymus

Ficus carica, Common Fig
Fuchsia 'Mrs. Lovell Swisher'
Fuchsia 'Rose of Castile'
Fuchsia magellanica riccartonii
Fuchsia magellanica,
  Firecracker Fuchsia
Fuchsia WH2 (serrated leaves)
Galium aparine
Gladiolus hybrid

Hebe franciscana
Hebe salicifolia
Hebe sp.
Hedera helix, English Ivy
Hedera helix variegata
Homeria breyniana
Hydrangea macrophylla,
  Big-leaf or Garden Hydrangea

Iris douglasiana, Douglas Iris
Iris spuria, Lilac-Flowered Iris
Iris sp., tall, bearded,
  several color morphs

Kniphofia uvaria, Red-hot Poker

Lathyrus latifolius,
  Perennial Sweet Pea
Lavatera arborea, Tree Mallow
Lavatera assurgentiflora, Malva Rosa
Leptospermum laevigatum,
  Australian Tea Tree

Leucojum aestivum, Snowflake
Ligustrum japonica, Japanese Privet
Lobularia maritima, Sweet Alyssum
Lonicera japonica,
    Japanese Honeysuckle
Lupinus arboreus, Bush Lupine

Maleophora crocea
Malus sp., Crabapple
Malva parviflora, Mallow
Mentha sp., Peppermint
Metrosideros excelsus,
    New Zealand Christmas Tree
Muscari armeniacum, Grape Hyacinth

Narcissus spp., several forms,
    including Paperwhites
Nothoscordum gracile, False Garlic

Olearia traversii
Oxalis pes-caprae, Bermuda Buttercup

Pelargonium 'California Brilliant'
Pelargonium 'Mrs. Langtry'

Pelargonium 'Our Frances'
Pelargonium 'San Antonio'
Pelargonium quercifolium
Pelargonium x domesticum
    'Prince Bismarck'
Pelargonium x hortorum
    'Alphonse Ricard'
Pittosporum crassifolium
Pittyrogramma triangularis
Polypodium scouleri,
    Leather Leaf Fern
Polypodium californicum,
    California Polypody Fern
Polystichum munitum,
    Western Sword Fern
Prunus cerasifera,
    Flowering Plum Tree
Prunus persica, Peach Tree
Pyracantha coccinea, Firethorn

Raphanus sativus, Wild Radish
Rhamnus californica, Coffeeberry
Rosa 'Blaze'
Rosa 'Dorothy Perkins'
Rosa 'Excelsa'
Rosa 'Félicité et Pérpetue'
Rosa 'Gardenia'
Rosa 'General MacArthur'
Rosa 'Gloire des Rosomanes'
Rosa 'Russeliana'
Rosa wichuraiana
Rubus sp., Blackberry

Schinus sp., Pepper Tree
Scrophularia californica, Figwort
Sedum dendroideum praealtum,
    Green Cockscomb
Senecio mikanioides,
    German Ivy
Sidalcea malvaeflora,
    Checker Mallow
Solanum americanum, Nightshade
Triteleia laxa (B. laxa),
    Ithuriel's Spear
Tropaeolum majus,
    Garden Nasturtium
Tulipa sp. (likely hybrid, leaves only),
    Tulips

Vinca major

Watsonia 'Mrs. Bullard's White'
Watsonia pyramidata, purple/pink
Watsonia species #1, soft orange
    tubular flower
Watsonia species #2, brilliant orange
    trumpet flower

Yucca aloifolia, Spanish Bayonet
Yucca gloriosa, Spanish Dagger

Zantedeschia aethiopica,
    Common Calla
Zauschneria cana,
    California Fuchsia,
    Hummingbird Flower

HEBE

Notes, Sources & Ackowledgements

THE ROCK GARDEN
John Hart

1. Compare John A. Martini's *Fortress Alcatraz*, 11, and James P. Delgado's *Alcatraz: Island of Change*, 9, for discussions of this translation.
2. See Frank M. Todd, *The Story of the Panama-Pacific International Exposition* (New York: Putnam's, 1921) for the larger account of this event.
3. Martini, *Fortress Alcatraz*, 117.
4. James P. Delgado & Associates, "Cultural Landscape Report for Alcatraz Island," 36.
5. Martini, *Fortress Alcatraz,* 117.
6. F. J. Clauss, *Alcatraz: Island of Many Mistakes*, 36.
7. Pierre Odier, *Alcatraz, The Rock: A History of Alcatraz, The Fort/The Prison*, 145.
8. Adam Fortunate Eagle, *Alcatraz! Alcatraz! The Indian Occupation of 1969-1971*, 16.
9. Fortunate Eagle, *Alcatraz! Alcatraz!*, 123.

In preparing this essay I have relied heavily on the writings of historian James P. Delgado, *Alcatraz: Island of Change* (San Francisco: Golden Gate National Park Association, 1991), *Alcatraz: The Story Behind the Scenery* (Las Vegas: KC Publications, 1985), and an unpublished document prepared by James P. Delgado & Associates, "Cultural Landscape Report for Alcatraz Island, Final Draft" (1992), available at Golden Gate National Recreation Area Headquarters, Fort Mason.

For the details of Alcatraz's development as a fortress, I have followed John A. Martini's excellent monograph, *Fortress Alcatraz: Guardian of the Golden Gate* (Kailua, Hawaii: Pacific Monograph, 1990).

These and indeed most recent writers about Alcatraz draw in turn on Erwin N. Thompson's massive survey, "The Rock: A History of Alcatraz Island, 1847-1972" (Denver: National Park Service, 1979), available in the National Maritime Museum at Fort Mason.

Pierre Odier's *Alcatraz, The Rock: A History of Alcatraz, The Fort/The Prison* (Eagle Rock, CA: L'image Odier, 1982) began as a project with the author's students at Herbert Hoover High School in Glendale, California. It is notably thorough and based on an impressive range of sources.

F. J. Clauss's *Alcatraz: Island of Many Mistakes* (Menlo Park, CA: Briarcliff Press, 1981) is a brief, readable synthesis.

Adam Fortunate Eagle's *Alcatraz! Alcatraz! The Indian Occupation of 1969-1971* (Berkeley, CA: Heyday Books/GGNPA, 1992) is a fascinating insider's view, partisan but fair-minded and credible.

In Robert Cameron's *Alcatraz* (San Francisco: Cameron and Co., 1989) the photographer offers a fine array of modern and historic photographs, catching the island at all angles and in all moods.

I've had the assistance of several park service professionals, including Daphne Hatch, John Martini, and Will Reyes. Thanks also to Michael Boland, Carlisle Becker, David de Sante, Mary Anne Stewart, and Peggy Wayburn.

LONG, ENDURING PATTERNS
Russell A. Beatty

Research for this manuscript began as a photographic search in the Presidio Museum, the San Francisco Maritime Museum, and the Bancroft Library at University of California at Berkeley for visual evidence of the gardens. Research on both the plants and history of the gardens was drawn heavily from the excellent work by Ron Lutsko and Robyn Menigoz, "The Historical Gardens of Alcatraz Island. Research for the Golden Gate National Park Association" (1992).

I also found Jolene Babyak's book, *Eyewitness on Alcatraz* (Berkeley, CA: Ariel Vamp Press, 1988) to be a valuable source of information, as were two works previously cited, Erwin Thompson's study, "The Rock: A History of Alcatraz Island, 1847-1972" (1979) and and John Martini's *Fortress Alcatraz*.

Detailed accounts of the gardens came from articles from the *San Francisco*

Chronicle, particularly "Trees Are Planted" (Feb. 8, 1924); John E. Bryan and Lynn MacInnis's article, "A Visit to Alcatraz, An Island of Contrasts" (*California Horticultural Journal* 35, 1974: 101-106); and correspondence in the files of both the San Francisco Maritime Museum and in the National Park Service office on Alcatraz: Robert C. Crabb, Information Memorandum Concerning: Endangered California Native Plants Installed on Alcatraz (January 11, 1984), Freddie Reichel, undated personal correspondence to Evelyn Strong, Site Supervisor, Alcatraz, and undated personal correspondence to the editor of an unidentified publication, and Mrs. Elmer M. Woodbury, First Annual Report and Future Plans, California Spring Blossom and Wild Flower Association (January 1924).

Elliott Michener, former inmate gardener, provided first-hand accounts of his experiences of a decade of gardening on Alcatraz; these details came in numerous letters to the author, particularly those of August 14 and August 26, 1995, as well as telephone conversations and a personal interview with the author (September 7, 1995, Sierra Madre, CA).

Information on the roses found on Alcatraz today came from a variety of published sources, including D. Austin, *Shrub Roses & Climbing Roses* (Suffolk, England: Antique Collectors Club, 1993); Jack Harkness, *Roses* (London: J. M. Dent & Sons Ltd., 1978); J. H. McFarland, *Modern Roses IV* (Harrisburg, PA: J. Horace McFarland Co., 1952); and G. A. Stevens, *Climbing Roses* (New York: The Macmillan Co., 1933), among others.

Information on the other Alcatraz plants came from Robyn Menigoz (personal interview with the author, 1995); Liberty Hyde and Ethel Zoe Bailey and the staff of the L. H. Bailey Hortorium, *Hortus Third* (New York: Macmillan Publishing Co., 1976); Charles A. Lewis, "Effects of Plants and Gardening in Creating Interpersonal and Community Well-Being" in *The Role of Horticulture in Human Well-Being and Social Development*, edited by Diane Relf (Portland, OR: Timber Press, 1992); and Richard Whitehall, "An Encounter with 'Ragged Robin'

 *Gardens of* ALCATRAZ

(*Pacific Horticulture* 54, no. 3, 1993: 15-19).

Researching the little-known topic of the gardens of Alcatraz required detective work not unlike the experience of the gardeners who scratched life out of the Rock and made it bloom. I am deeply indebted to the following peope who helped make this story bloom as well.

Landscape architect Robyn Menigoz for accompanying me on several delightful field trips to the island; landscape architect Ron Lutsko, without whose detailed inventory any understanding of the plants and layers of plantings would have been impossible; friend, rosarian, and horticulturist Bob Cowden, who helped me discover the background of the roses of Alcatraz and the stories they tell; National Park Service employees Dennis Copeland for opening the photo archives at the Presidio Museum (where I found the photograph of Elliott Michener), Will Reyes and other rangers on Alcatraz for allowing me to explore the island, Alcatraz ranger Lori Thomsen, who made possible the fortuitous connection with Elliott Michener; Elliott Michener himself, for his generosity and openness in sharing his remarkable experiences, ones that changed his life and touched mine; editor Susan Tasaki, whose editing skill made a long text more readable by hard pruning; the late Freddie Reichel, who recorded his Alcatraz gardening memories in 1978; and to all the other gardeners of Alcatraz who proved that gardening makes both plants and people bloom.

PARADISE RECLAIMED
Michael Boland

In preparing this essay, I relied substantially on information gathered during ongoing Alcatraz planning and design efforts (1991 through 1995). Among these projects was the development of an overall island plan and the construction of a new trail along the island's southern edge. As did the authors of the other essays, I found James Delgado's "Cultural

Landscape Report of Alcatraz, Final Draft" (1992) and Lutsko Associates' excellent condition assessment of the gardens, "The Historical Gardens of Alcatraz Island" (1992) particularly useful.

A number of general studies of the island's wildlife have been conducted, and information on this topic was gleaned from many sources. For this work, I relied most heavily on William Boarman's "The Breeding Birds of Alcatraz Island: Life on the Rock" (1989) and Judd Howell and Tania Pollack's "Alcatraz as a Wildlife Refuge" (1991). For more detailed information on the island's significant western gull population I depended primarily on a series of studies by Douglas Bell, especially "Alcatraz Island Western Gull Nest Survey" (1990), and Raymond Pierotti and Cynthia Annett's "Management of the Western Gull Colony in Relation to the Open Island Concept on Alcatraz Island" (1989). Detailed data on the black-crowned night herons came from a number of studies conducted by the National Park Service, and the San Francisco Bird Observatory's "Black-Crowned Night Heron Nesting Study" (1990). All of these unpublished reports and studies are located in the files of the Resource Management Division, Golden Gate National Recreation Area.

Over the years, I have had the assistance and support of too many National Park Service staff to name—but special thanks go to Doug Nadeau, Nancy Hornor, Nick Weeks, Daphne Hatch, and the ranger staff on Alcatraz. Most importantly, I would like to thank Greg Moore for that first memorable trip to Alcatraz some five years ago.

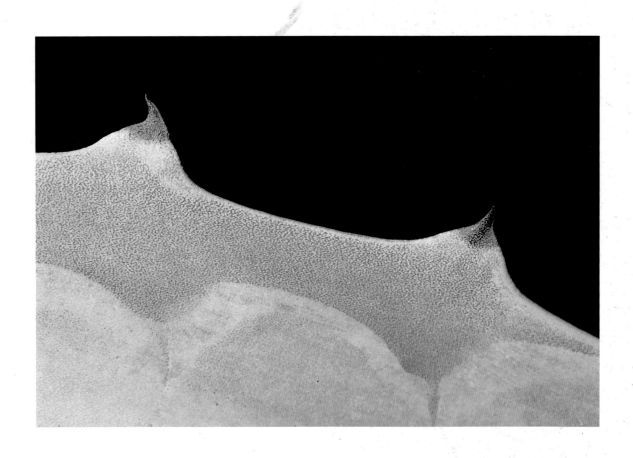